THE THIRD REICH

THE THIRD REICH

Its Beginnings

Its Development

Its End

BY HANS BUCHHEIM

KÖSEL-VERLAG, MUNICH

Translated by Allan and Lieselotte Yahraes

Originally published in Germany under the title
"Das Dritte Reich". © 1958 by Kösel-Verlag, Munich
Second English Edition
© 1961 by Kösel-Verlag, Munich. Printed in Germany
Produced by Graphische Werkstätten Kösel, Kempten

On January 30, 1933, Reichs President von Hindenburg appointed Adolf Hitler Reichs Chancellor. With that act the President entrusted the leadership of the German state to a man who had never made a secret of his hostility toward the Weimar Republic. On the contrary, he had consistently used techniques designed to destroy the Republic, techniques that did a great deal to bring about the crisis that it was now hoped he would master.

Although the event took place in a framework of legalism, the German public rightly saw it as a break with the past, and awaited far-going changes, whether for better or for worse. Within this general state of mind, there was a widespread readiness among even the democratically-minded citizenry to "give Hitler a chance". The economic crisis and the chronic ineffectiveness of the Reichstag had made many Germans republic-weary, and had strengthened others in their outright opposition to the Weimar Republic. Meanwhile, only the smallest fraction of the public had enough power of political imagination to be able to foresee the kind of consequences that would follow an elimination of constitutional guarantees and the disbanding of the democratic system. Another factor at work was a skillfully-fostered national consciousness.

The start of Hitler's regime was characterized

as a "national awakening". It took its appropriate symbolism from a ceremony of state at Potsdam on March 21, 1933: There, at the grave of Frederick the Great, Hindenburg – who was more Field Marshal of the old Prussia than he was President of the Republic – shook the hand of a deferentially bowing Hitler. New fuel was fed to the old prejudices that democratic thinking and national thinking were incompatible. Violations of the democratic constitution were nothing to worry about (so went the prejudice) as long as the violations served national goals. Wide circles of the public unblinkingly accepted actions of national-minded men (as well as of men who were considered national-minded) that, had the same actions been undertaken by Communists, would have been considered alarming violations of justice and order. In the week following the Reichstag elections of March 5, when the black-white-red flag was hoisted on the city halls of German communities,[1] the impression made by this national demonstration found only a few alert to the unconstitutionality of the act; and most people also overlooked the significance of the revolutionary red of the swastika flag flying at the side of the other flag. It took bitter experience to teach most of the public that they had started down a road along which they would see

[1] The flag of the Weimar Republic was black-red-gold.

the destruction of not only the democratic constitution but also every legal commitment of the state itself. Nor did most suspect that this seemingly "national" movement would in truth inflict severe damage on the nation.

In the new so-called "cabinet of national concentration", eight "bourgeois-national" ministers (as distinguished from National Socialist nationalists) faced only three National Socialist ministers, one of them Hitler himself. Papen had in mind this voting relationship within the Cabinet when he arranged for Hitler's nomination as Chancellor. Thus Papen did not doubt that he could make use of the political energies of the National Socialist movement, and yet keep in his own hands the decision about the course to be taken – did not doubt, in other words, that he could remain master of the situation. For Hitler, on the other hand, the "national awakening" meant nothing less than a seizure of power. He firmly intended to reorganize the state according to his own concepts, and to bend it to his political purposes. That is why the distribution of votes in the Cabinet was more or less a matter of indifference to him. For him, the decisive factor was to get the apparatus of the executive power into his hands. He had seen that the existence of the modern state has become so dependent upon its administrative apparatus – that is to say, upon its technical organization – that this apparatus can paralyze the state's legal and political functioning, its constitution, its government. Thus indirect alterations of the constitution via the administrative route became a typical phenomenon of the Third Reich: The most unlikely decree and the most innocuous-appearing assignment of competences might contain the germ of some revolutionary alteration of the constitution. Furthermore, as Hitler did not shrink from breaking his word and from the use of force, he was able to cow his cabinet within a short time; as early as October 1934 the Reich ministers had to swear an oath of loyalty and allegiance to him.

The decisive act of the consolidation of power was neither the narrow Reichstag election victory of the government coalition of March 5 nor the Enabling Act that was passed on March 23, 1933, by which the parliament renounced its participation in law-making. It was rather the so-called "Decree of the Reichs President for the Protection of People and State". It was issued on February 28 of that year, one day after the burning of the Reichstag – an event which was represented as the opening gun of a Communist conspiracy that was allegedly in the making. This decree served nominally to protect the state against Communist-engendered acts of violence, but it was in reality Hitler's instrument for speedily checkmating all his political opponents, and for reducing the German states (*Länder*) to a common level of subjection. To begin with, it abolished the basic rights as guaranteed in the Weimar constitution. In the second place, it ordained that the government of the Reich could take over the police power in those states that, in the opinion of the Reich government, had not undertaken the necessary measures for the "restoration of public security and order". This significant decree was never lifted, but remained to form the basis of the absolute police power with which Hitler surrounded his rulership. It exploited the leeway provided for in Article 48 of the Constitution of the Reich without at the same time taking into account the qualifications or security provisions that were also laid down there. Thus the decree put Germany into a permanent state of emergency. Every legal safeguard was lifted to the degree that suited the purposes of the state's leadership. Much later, during the war years, the Gestapo was still citing the decree of February 28, 1933, as authority for arrests. The decree served, too, when the regime arrested members of the Protestant and Catholic clergy on the ground that they were delivering political sermons that stirred up unrest and served as a starting point for Communist elements to endanger the security of people and state – this at a time when Hitler was making a pact with Soviet Russia.

From the day of the seizure of power onward, terror and violence accompanied the misuse of the emergency clauses of the Constitution. Political foes of the regime and Jews were bullied, beaten, locked up, and indeed in quite a few cases brutally killed. Those scholars, publicists, artists who were not in favor were pushed out of their positions and many had to flee abroad. Throughout the Reich the SA (Brown Shirts) established concentration camps, where it wrought revenge on its enemies undisturbed by the police.

In 1934 the camps were taken over by the SS. They were organized by regular bureaucratic methods as permanent establishments. Their purpose was to demoralize and eliminate real and alleged enemies of the Third Reich. From 1942 onward, this political goal receded into the background and an economic one took precedence: The whole area of Greater Germany was overlaid with a net of compulsory-labor camps, in which prisoners from all the nations of the occupied part of Europe worked for SS-run enterprises or otherwise for the financial gain of the SS.

Behind the so-called policy of co-ordination of the year 1933 was the desire to transfer the political principles of the party organization to every area of public life, and to subject everything to centralized control. One of the most important of these measures followed the abolition of the trade unions on May 2, 1933. German labor was organized as the "German Labor Front". With this act was connected the attempt to basically reorganize employer-employee relations and to give the worker a new status in the community – at first glance, in fact, a change in his life for the better. The old employer and employee organizations were replaced by a concept of the enterprise as a community of interests and a partnership of production. Workers received wage and pension guarantees. Moreover, a propagandistic stress on the moral value of work ("Work ennobles") was supposed to raise the worker's prestige in society and build up his self-confidence.

Very soon, however, these advantages proved to be a burdensome mortgage to the worker within the developing totalitarian system. Not that he was burdened by the private entrepreneur, who now found himself theoretically on a par with his employees. The worker's new sense of being oppressed stemmed rather from the policy of the regime. Previously, he had had to worry about making a living. But now he found himself under the moral compulsion to prove himself worthy of the privileges that were held out to him as a reward for accomplishment. Inferior work performance was no longer a private affair that meant merely a cutback in the worker's personal standard of living. Falling down on the job now became "sabotage of the Führer's work of construction" – sabotage that even in the prewar years was made a political offense. Thus it was that even when the "Labor Front" brought social reforms that in themselves were welcome, they turned out to be a very mixed blessing. The reforms ended up to the worker's disadvantage, because the new ways had been thought out not from solicitude for his welfare, but simply in order to bolster the potential strength of the state.

This "co-ordination" by the regime passed over certain organizations, at least at first. The groups that were least affected by it were institutions that could make a political contribution of their own. Such institutions by and large disposed of an internal order that had been hardened by tradition, and that had not been deeply affected by the previous years during which the German nation underwent the processes of democratization. These groups included the armed forces, the ministerial bureaucracies, the churches, and those areas of the economy that were the domains either of "bourgeois" and nationally-oriented citizenry or of the aristocracy. It is true that an effort at "co-ordination" was attempted within the churches in 1933. But it did not make headway; and the churches remained one of Hitler's unsolved problems until the end. As for the other institutionalized groups mentioned above, Hitler shrewdly avoided chancing a fight with them. Instead he sought to win their loyalty through tactical compromises, which were possible as long as he could make them think that he served their interests. He chose to wear them down, and with their own help gradually to create a situation in which they could no longer exert their power against him, but had only the choice of obeying or being eliminated.

These tactics were, however, seriously thrown off their course as early as the autumn of 1933 – by the brown-shirted SA. Now that Hitler had come to power, the SA understandably enough wanted a say in the coming reorganization of the German nation. For a few months it was permitted to vent its fury on its opponents, but, under the leadership of Röhm, it wanted something more. It showed social-revolutionary aspirations. Moreover, the SA wanted to become an actual part of the new regime, to a degree corresponding to its power. It sought recognition as a people's army of National Socialism, serving first alongside and later, as its leadership hoped, in place of the regular armed forces, the Reichswehr. This was a demand that Hitler was flatly not prepared to grant. First of all, his position of power was not yet so well-grounded that he dared risk a falling-out with the Reichswehr, especially not so long as Hindenburg was still alive. And secondly, his plans in the field of foreign policy made it impossible for him to do away with an army that was a first-rate military arm. Particularly indispensable to him was the officers' corps, whose effectiveness it would have taken decades to build up anew.

So Hitler had to scheme to eliminate the SA as a factor of power. With this goal in mind, he did nothing at first to ease the frictions that were accumulating between the Reichswehr and the SA, or to stem the rising tide of mutual animosity. Instead, he let things drift long enough to be sure that the Reichswehr would not only tolerate a *coup* against the SA, but would even greet it with relief. This *coup* took place on June 30, 1934. Overnight, proven and powerful SA leaders went down as "perverts" and "traitors". Overnight the SA itself collapsed, at a single blow, into a mass organization without influence and without a political profile. This achievement by the state involved hundredfold murder. This in turn opened the eyes of many Germans who until then had followed political and economic developments with a certain attitude of benevolence. As for the National Socialist Party, the NSDAP, among its adherents too, there were many cases of disappointment and disillusionment. But there was also another reaction. As the highly illegal act against the SA had hit precisely those persons who up to now had been proponents of illegality, many individuals deluded themselves with the thought that the regime had simply extirpated an element that had not fitted into the over-all picture of a civilized movement of national awakening. This solacing interpretation was an utter misjudgment of the situation.

For the truth was that Hitler had seized his chance to get rid of, not only some elements of social-revolutionary unrest, but also those "bourgeois national" politicians who might have become a danger to him. The 30th of June, 1934, was the beginning of the end of the attempt to cast the National Socialist regime in a conservative mold. In fact, this stylization lasted only until the Gestapo established, besides its special section for dealing with "Communism and Marxism", another to deal with "reaction and rightist opposition".

Before 1933, many Germans had sympathized with Hitler because they could not imagine the degree to which he would misuse his power. Later, when he was at the apex of his might, most persons lacked the possibility of doing anything effective to counter his criminal policies. But between January 30, 1933, and Hindenburg's death on

August 2, 1934, Hitler had already shown clearly enough what sort of man he was. Nor was he so firmly in the saddle that he could not have been overthrown. During this period, if only a part of the most prominent officials, men of learning, officers and intellectuals had decided to stage a demonstrative protest, Hitler by no means would have been able to hold his ground. That these individuals failed at this point to take such a step is the most tangible evidence of the political complicity of the German citizenry and the nobility in the National Socialist regime.

The Reichswehr, too, although it kept itself out of the wave of murders of SA leaders, obviously did not understand the signs of the times. On the contrary, the armed forces believed themselves the victors in the affair, secure once and for all in their status as "the sole bearer of arms for the nation". Within the Reichswehr, not enough political imagination was exercised in order to grasp the importance of an event that took place on the very day on which the army was freed of competition from the SA. On that day, Sepp Dietrich received Hitler's word that the "life guards" would be organized as a regiment with modern armament. Thus that day was the birthday of the SS alert troops, which later became the armed SS. The SS began to contest the primacy of the army, not in a clumsy head-on attack, but step by step, moving cautiously. The new armed units were free of any long-standing political or ideological traditions. They lived and breathed National Socialism. They knew no other possibility than "loyalty to the Führer". For them, there would be no conflict between obedience to Hitler and responsibility to the nation.

But the leadership of the Reichswehr did not see through the fact that Hitler had emasculated the SA, not in order to allow the traditional powers behind the state to thrive undisturbed, but rather to keep them from becoming suspicious. Far from seeing through Hitler, the Reichswehr leaders, in a naive spirit of gratitude, offered their co-operation a short time later in a stroke of first importance and of immeasurable consequences: After Hindenburg's death the Reichswehr leadership failed to insist upon a constitutional decision about his successor, but instead agreed that the entire armed forces would take an oath to Hitler as the new chief of state. The Reichswehr swore to God its unconditional loyalty to the person of Hitler – and by doing so affected its own future in two ways. First, the armed forces lost what political independence and freedom of action they had had. Secondly, they burdened every single German in uniform with a potential conflict of conscience: between the duty to obey an individual and the duty to uphold the common welfare.

After Hitler made himself head of the German state on August 2, 1934, there was no longer any legal and political authority except his own. He was free to transform his role from that of a power within the state to that of a power over the state. He was free to use that power as an instrument of his foreign-policy plans. Here his goal at first was the same as that of the governments of the Weimar Republic: the revision of the Treaty of Versailles. But his basic approach was quite different.

Hitler's predecessors in the office of Chancellor, at least up to Brüning, had worked for the restoration of Germany's rights while all the while taking for granted the interdependence of the nations of Europe. These earlier Chancellors felt obligated to do nothing that in the foreseeable future might threaten a new armed conflict among the European peoples. But not Hitler. On the contrary, he took advantage of any breach in European solidarity, and he made capital out of Europe's worry about a new war. He disregarded the common interests of the European family of peoples. He gambled on the individual weaknesses and particular interests of the various nations. He did not hesitate to poison the international climate with acts of gross dishonesty, nor was he afraid to foster the continuous threat of a European war. Using such methods, he was able, it is true, to achieve shining triumphs within a short time – gains that the democratic statesmen would not have made so quickly. But he paid for the gains by torpedoing the movement, just then getting under way, toward more stable relationships in Europe. Finally, Hitler did not even hesitate to pave a road for Russia right into the heart of the European continent, doing so through his pact with the Soviet Union. The argument often advanced in defense of such a policy – namely, that other nations had acted no differently a hundred years or more ago – offered a justification more apparent than real. In reality, historical developments during the first third of the 20th Century had already reached a new stage. The German future was too closely linked with the European future for anyone to attain genuine and lasting successes for Germany at the expense of Europe.

When Hitler took over the government, good progress had already been made on the revision of the Treaty of Versailles. The Conference of Lausanne in the summer of 1932 had practically brought an end to payments of reparations. By decision of the disarmament conference of December 11 of the same year, Germany in principle had been granted equal rights in questions of armament. True enough, in this field in particular much time and patience would still have been needed in order to arrive at concrete conclusions. But the prospects were good, especially as a goodly part of the American sympathy for France had gone glimmering because of the inflexible French attitude and because France had stopped payments on her debts.

At first, on May 17, 1933, Hitler made a foreign-policy address that showed a very moderate attitude. He evoked hopes abroad that Germany would co-operate in future international negotiations. But then, on October 14, he brusquely announced the withdrawal of Germany from the disarmament conference and from the League of Nations. Yet at the same time he could show considerable success in negotiations with two powers that one would have thought the Third Reich least ready to come to terms with. On July 20 the Concordat was concluded with the Holy See. And on November 15 the first communiqués were issued about a German-Polish mutual accommodation. It was to culminate in the agreement of January 26, 1934. Particular astonishment was aroused by this understanding with Poland, the only country with which the Weimar Republic had known serious tensions. The news of the Polish-German pact seemed to remove any possibility to doubt the sincerity of Hitler's desire for peace – even though he clearly wanted to go his own way. Incidentally, this treaty demonstrated what sort of blank checks the German people were ready to hand to "nationally minded men". For a democratic government that would have dared to risk a Polish settlement that included a renunciation of the Corridor would have been torn apart. And Hitler would have been at the head of the list of those doing their utmost to revile such an act of "treason" and such a "sell-out".

A basic characteristic of Hitler's foreign-policy tactics became apparent in these first months: He shrank from multilateral obligations, from treaties and pacts in which he would have had to deal with a number of partners at the same time. He shunned all agreements that were backed by the guarantees of several different powers. He liked to negotiate with only one partner at a time. His aim was bilateral treaties, the keeping of which he would have to argue about with only one lone contracting party. His method served a policy that had no intention of keeping within the European framework. On the contrary, he sought to separate every nation individually, one after the other, from this community. In this regard Hitler had great success. While Western diplomacy was striving for European collective security, and increasingly so from the summer of 1934 onward, Hitler moved in the opposite direction. Poland was not the only nation that he dissuaded from joining in a collective European security arrangement. France in particular was trying to include Germany and the Soviet Union in a system of non-aggression pacts in Eastern Europe like those that already existed in the West under the Locarno pact. Hitler, however, avoided getting into this scheme, which would have curbed his freedom of action in Eastern Europe. Instead of signing pacts in the East, he waited for a good opening to escape from contractual ties in the West.

He saw one such opening in the reintroduction in France of a two-year term of military service. On March 16, 1935, he declared that the Versailles Treaty's armaments restrictions on Germany were void, and he introduced universal conscription. This move brought a reaction from England, France and Italy in April of the same year. They announced that they would oppose with all suitable means each and every unilateral cancellation of a treaty. But only a few months passed before this so-called "Stresa Front" turned out to be a very weak bulwark indeed. Hitler's gamble on the failure of European solidarity paid off: On June 18, 1935, England concluded a naval agreement with Germany. By so doing, England recognized the German policy of revisionism, and also Germany's treaty violation that the British had opposed so strongly a short time previously. This was the first step in a policy of concessions that England pursued until the Polish crisis in

1939. This policy expressed the fact that Europe had both a bad conscience over the Versailles Treaty and little experience in handling totalitarian regimes. Now there was a readiness to revise all situations that obviously violated the principle of popular self-determination. Life had been made unnecessarily hard for the German statesmen who before 1933 had honestly worked for a peaceful order in Europe; now the path was being smoothed for a man who used revisionism merely as a starting-point toward much bigger goals.

On October 3, 1935, Italy began her war against Ethiopia. The sanctions that England and France halfheartedly decreed were not enough to seriously threaten the Italian campaign – but were, however, enough to strain the good relations among the "Stresa states", and, moreover, to badly damage the reputation of the League of Nations. Meanwhile Hitler, on his side, gave generous political and material support to Italy, and brought about a decisive turn in Italo-German relations. Up to now, Mussolini had determinedly opposed all of Hitler's ambitions in Southeast Europe, and had frustrated Hitler's attempt to annex Austria by means of a *putsch* in 1934. From 1936 onward, however, Mussolini exhibited understanding for Germany's interest in Austria. Thus the Ethiopian war created the soil out of which were to grow both the "Berlin–Rome Axis" and the Austrian *Anschluss.*

But before those developments came about, Mussolini offered Hitler the chance to take, more or less within the Italian dictator's protecting shadow, the most daring step of his whole political career. On March 7, 1936, Hitler announced Germany's withdrawal from the system of mutual guarantees that the West had set up at Locarno, and he sent German troops marching into the demilitarized zone of the Rhineland. German armament at that time was still at such a state of development that not even a joint action by the Western Powers, but merely the energetic intervention of France would have been needed to force Hitler into a humiliating retreat. This Hitler himself later admitted; and he called the 48 hours after the marching orders the most exciting of his life. But France could not decide to mobilize, and England did nothing to encourage her. The two powers showed that they were not ready to act in support of the order they themselves had created. So it was that they let pass the last opportunity to bring Hitler to a standstill with a relatively small military engagement. And on the other hand, who wanted to sacrifice peace only so as to keep Germany from disposing for herself over her western border areas? At the same time, who was able to predict what was to come, and to predict it so conclusively as to justify starting a war? At that time, all of Hitler's moves were at one and the same time a restoration of German rights and the preparation for a heedless policy of expansion; it was this duality that made it so difficult to take appropriate counter-action. One consequence of the German entry into the Rhineland was to weaken severely the French system of alliances, especially that of the Little Entente. France's partners in the Little Entente drew dark conclusions about her readiness to come to their aid in case of need, now that she had not even stood up in defense of her own interests. Hitler, on the other hand, had gotten what he needed to erect the military screen known as the *Westwall* (Siegfried Line).

Hitler himself once called the year 1936 "the year of the hard decisions". That applied not only to the occupation of the demilitarized zone. It also referred to the decision made in the summer of that year to approach the "problem of German living space". For Hitler, to do something about *Lebensraum* meant to switch from a policy of gambling on Europe's fear of war to a policy of actual preparation for war. Hitler was convinced that Germany had to have more *Lebensraum* if the Germans were to be self-sufficient – independent of other nations, and especially of the fluctuations of the world market. Nor should this "living space", as Hitler saw it, be overseas where hostile nations could cut off access to it at any time; he wanted it to be an area immediately adjoining Germany, and he saw it in the East. Hitler was furthermore convinced that Germany could not choose her own time to prepare for the conquest of the *Lebensraum,* but had to make use of the years in which the world was not yet sufficiently armed to take effective counter-measures. Accordingly, he saw the period of 1943–1945 as the last possible time at which to launch the "unavoidable" war.

Given these circumstances, the major decision that had to be made did not concern rearmament. This was being pushed as fast as possible anyway. The problem was economic. Hitler's plan was to make Germany as economically autarchic as he could in preparation for the years from the onset of war until the newly-won areas could be exploited. He was ready to pay for success with maximum temporary sacrifice and with economic retrenchment. The big task was not so much how to make sure of a food supply, but how to utilize German mineral resources to the utmost and how to produce gasoline, rubber and fibres synthetically. But by 1936 the growth of the German economy had started to taper off. If normal foreign trade were to be carried on, and if only reasonable things were to be expected of the national production rate, then further growth would be going uphill. Specifically, it appeared as if it would take more years to reach the hoped-for national autarchy than Hitler felt he had at his disposal.

So Hitler made this decision in 1936: to plunge ahead into an economic policy that would deliberately cut adrift from relatively normal economic circumstances. While the crash program was to speed up Germany's readiness for war, at the same time it hung for its success on an enlargement of the *Lebensraum* within a few years – otherwise the scheme would collapse. This was the meaning of the "Four Years Plan" announced in 1936. In the official text, it is true, the real meaning could be read only between the lines. But it came out more clearly in Hitler's "Memorandum on the Four Years Plan", which ends with the words: "Accordingly I set the following task: 1. The German army must be ready for action in 4 years. 2. The German economy must be ready for war in 4 years."

With the launching of the Four Years Plan, the German economy began to lose its relative independence of Hitler. To be sure, it had been serving his policy all the while, but it had done so while remaining loyal to its own procedures and interests. Within this balance of interests, Schacht, both as president of the Reichsbank and as Minister of Economics, had devoted his talent ever since 1933 to accomplishing for Hitler anything within the realm of the possible. The surprising politico-economic successes of the Third Reich's early years were due in large part to Schacht. He had not always acted correctly and fairly toward other countries, but he had always known what he was about. Schacht had a notion comparable to that of Papen when the latter thought he could keep Hitler in hand through the voting ratio in the Cabinet. As Schacht saw it, Hitler held out the promise of something the German business world urgently desired: a stable government. At the same time – so thought Schacht – Hitler would be reined in by the laws of economics themselves. He obviously did not believe simply that Hitler would be capable of acting against all economic reason, and would be able to pursue with wide-open eyes a policy that could be leading only to inflation or to war. In 1936, Göring courageously marched in where wise men might have feared to tread, and took on the responsibility for making the Four Years Plan work. Inevitably there were frictions between him and Schacht. The latter tried for a time to steer the old course; but in November, 1937, he got out by resigning from the Ministry of Economics.

At home, Hitler's efforts in 1936 and 1937 were directed at enlarging Germany's potential; abroad, at finding friends. In the latter effort, he was aided by the huge success of the Olympic Games in Berlin as a manoeuvre in prestige. The games won back for Germany surprisingly much foreign sympathy – good will that had been lost since 1933 by Hitler's violent domestic and foreign policies. Obviously there was willingness in wide circles beyond Germany's borders to admire Hitler's successes, without inquiring too much about the price tag or about his future plans. Then too, the Spanish civil war gave Hitler the opportunity of intensifying his political partnership with Italy. It also gave him one ally more, in Franco – who could perhaps turn out to be useful along France's border, or in the hinterland of England's fortress at Gibraltar.

During the month of October 1936 the German-Italian relationship took on tangible shape. In November, Mussolini coined for it the term "Berlin–Rome Axis". Meanwhile German diplomacy was making its bid for European sympathy by representing Germany as Europe's bulwark and champion against "the world-wide menace of Communism". This anti-Bolshevist theme had already been sounded at the Nuremberg party rally in September. The campaign made its mark. In November 1936 the Anti-Comintern Pact was concluded between Germany and Japan. Officially, it provided only for exchange of informations on the activity of the Communist Internationale. But in a secret supplement to the pact there were provisions for an alliance against Soviet Russia.

The first months of 1938 brought more events the highest significance of which was scarcely noticed by the public. The Reich War Minister and commander-in-chief of the armed forces, Field Marshal von Blomberg, had married on January 12 for the second time. Just a few days later it became known that his new wife had previously been under the supervision of the section of the police that had to do with prostitutes. When this got out, Blomberg had to resign. With the impact of this scandal still fresh, people felt that there might be very well something in a second scandal: a slander against the commander-in-chief of the army, General von Fritsch, to the effect that he practiced homosexual relations. Given the public mood of credibility, Hitler was able to keep the suspicion alive, even though the unjustly accused Fritsch had offered to make a statement on his word of honor. He also submitted to a humiliating confrontation with a man who had several times previously been convicted on charges of homosexuality. And Fritsch also agreed to being interrogated by the Gestapo, which up to then had had no authority at all within the world of the armed forces. In the end, before a court of honor had brought in a finding, Hitler dismissed the army commander-in-chief.

So it was that the name of Blomberg lent itself to one of Hitler's skillful manoeuvres. The armed services had already been politically "coordinated"; now they lost their professional military independence. Hitler made himself the commander-in-chief, and readied, for his own occupancy, the office of top strategist in a coming war. The ministerial prerogatives of the Reich War Ministry were done away with. The newly established "High Command of the Armed Forces" was Hitler's military staff – nothing but a technical outfit without autonomy. Along with these decisions came another: On February 4, 1938, it was announced that Ribbentrop had been appointed as Reich Foreign Minister. Up to then he had been "Special Commissioner of the Führer" for matters of foreign policy. He was a devoted Hitlerite, without capacity or will for concepts of his own. That move brought the German diplomatic service, too, under Hitler's direct influence.

Nor was that all. The resignation of Schacht as Minister of Economics was followed by the appointment of Funk, on February 7, 1938. How little influence this man was intended to have can be deduced from the fact that he was not even introduced into his new duties until the commissioner for the Four Years Plan, Göring, first had reorganized the ministry. Thus Hitler's tactics now turned to the field of economics. The previously responsible ministry was degraded to a mere administrative unit, carrying out orders; the policy decisions became the job of Hitler's special commissioner. Here again the tendency under Hitler became clear: to curb the power and influence of the traditional administrative bodies. From now on, this tendency was to gain ground rapidly. Every ministry went through a similar process of atrophy. The Ministry of the Interior faded out in favor of the SS. The Ministry of Culture had to give precedence to the HJ (Hitler Youth); and the Labor Ministry to Gauleiter Sauckel's office of the commissioner general for planned distribution of labor.

After the decisions of 1936 and the new events of January and February 1938 came the *Anschluss* of Austria to the Reich, on March 12 of the same year. True, it was welcomed even by many non-National Socialist Germans as the fulfilment of an old longing, and it was accepted by non-German nations as a right long withheld from the Germans. But in reality this act belonged to the category of Hitler's developing policy of aggression, and as such the Austrian *Anschluss* did not correspond to Germany's true interests. It was on February 12 that Hitler and Schuschnigg met on the Obersalzberg. Then and there the Austrian

Federal Chancellor felt forced to say yes to the so-called Berchtesgaden Agreement. It provided for close foreign-policy and military ties between the two nations, and the participation of Austrian National Socialists in the Austrian government. Schuschnigg tried on March 8 to save his country's independence by calling for a plebiscite on short notice; whereupon Hitler forced him to resign, on March 11. During the following night German troops began to occupy Austria. Against the general jubilation in Austria and the satisfaction in Germany, scruples over the methods that Hitler had used and worry about what he would do next counted for little.

Encouraged by his success, Hitler began at once to get ready to deal with Czechoslovakia. As early as the end of March 1938 he gave his instructions to Konrad Henlein, the leader of the Sudeten German Party. Henlein was always to demand so much in his negotiations with the Prague government that his demands could not be satisfied. Meanwhile, the international configuration was favorable for Hitler. England let it be known that she did not wish to enter into obligations vis-a-vis Prague. Thereupon France had to make the fulfilment of her own commitments depend to a large extent on whether she could reckon on the help of the Soviet Union. But the Soviet Union, in order to interfere, would

33

have had to march through territory of Poland and Rumania – a move that these two nations were unwilling to permit. Thus the Prague government saw itself more or less on its own. When the situation had already reached an extremely serious stage, however, the British Prime Minister, Mr. Chamberlain, tried for a settlement by his personal intervention. On the one hand, he sought to learn Hitler's conditions for renouncing a military action that would have meant the end of the Czech state and possibly a European war. On the other hand, Mr. Chamberlain hoped to get the Czechs to accept Hitler's conditions. But Hitler refused to commit himself to definite demands; he impeded every discussion by showing increased impatience and irritability. "Three hundred Sudeten Germans have been killed. Things cannot go on like that. The affair has to be settled right away. I am determined to settle it; I do not care whether there is to be a world war or not." So he exclaimed during his first conference with Chamberlain on the Obersalzberg on September 15. Chamberlain declared his readiness to recommend to the Prague government the cession of the Sudeten German territories. But when at the beginning of his second meeting with Hitler, in Bad Godesberg on September 22, he brought word that the Czechs had decided to accept Hitler's demands, Hitler set new conditions: concerning

34

the procedures and the time-tables for handing over the conceded territories. He wanted to do away with Czechoslovakia altogether; and the more concessions that were made to him to prevent this, the more irritable he became. He finally presented his new conditions in a memorandum, an ultimatum. It was rejected by Prague, and now the way to a solution by force seemed to lie open. At that point, England succeeded in the eleventh hour to bring in Mussolini – whose renewed efforts at mediation Hitler did not dare to torpedo. Thus the Munich Conference of September 29 and 30 came about. In the main, the conferees accepted Hitler's new demands. Europe sighed in relief. Once again, war had been avoided. People hoped that Hitler was now satiated, and peace secured for years to come.

In Germany, those who warned against a policy of irresponsible gambling had once again been put in the wrong. Hitler obviously had known better than they how much could be demanded of Europe. Anyone who sought to reproach him for his lack of a feeling for European oneness would have been confronted by the behavior of Poland. She allowed herself to make use of the favorable opportunity of taking the Teschen area from Czechoslovakia, on October 10. Once more Hitler had demonstrated what success an unscrupulous venture can bring; luck was with him even in situations where there had seemed to be no way out. Through such developments, he won from many, including some of the cool-headed among the Germans, a reputation for infallibility. He began far and wide to be credited with a capacity for judgment that bordered on the miraculous; it seemed superior to that of any critic who operated merely on a basis of common sense. This wonderment at Hitler had an after-effect in times of his most serious setbacks and most obviously wrong decisions. For by then Hitler's reputation as a master-mind worked to paralyze initiative and the courage to resist him. Even in quite hopeless situations, the awe that Hitler had won prevented the formation of any general conviction that Germany was being steered toward disaster. This was the secret of Hitler's various successes: that in case after case he knew how to go all the way. He inflated each new demand, and his concept of his right to make that demand to such proportions that he steeled himself to stake everything on having his way. This all-out determination was for him a source of immense energy. In order to achieve each and every limited purpose, he risked everything. And as long as his opponents, in seeking to hinder him, shrank from the same attitude of all-out commitment, they kept losing to him. On each new occasion, Hitler saw the world from the angle of his latest purpose. He knew how to take the demand toward which he had just directed his attention, and raise it to the central point in the universe. Once having managed to do so, he could glance at the actual, existing conditions, and find them insignificant. Later the reverse side of the coin appeared. For the more this reality that Hitler held in contempt forced itself upon him, the more his will hastened Germany's downfall. That is to say, when the will power he had exerted to bring about the ascendancy of the German Reich ran up against hard facts, the will power became monomania, became illusion; and the nation toppled.

As early as December 17, 1938, Hitler instructed the armed forces to occupy "the rest of Czechoslovakia", in which he had claimed to be uninterested. His supposed lack of interest in the territory was the basis of the Munich agreements, and as recently as on September 26 he had sought to sound reassuring, in a speech on the subject ("We certainly don't want any Czechs!"). Now, however, Hitler found it relatively simple to create a situation ripe for his intervention. He fostered the Slovakian drive for autarchy. Under German pressure, Slovakia declared itself an independent state, on March 14, 1939. Thereupon the Czechoslovakian President, Mr. Hacha, traveled to Berlin, that same day, to have a personal talk with Hitler, to save what could be saved. But he came as the representative of a broken nation, unsupported by the powers of Europe. So he could not do but agree to make to the world an explanation dictated by Hitler: that the Czech leader was placing the destiny of the Czech people trustingly in the hands of the Führer of the German Reich. Even before his words were out, German troops had started the march toward Prague. A few days later, Hitler required Lithuania to return the Memel district, a move that had been under preparation for several months.

The annexation of Czechoslovakia was relatively easy and without risk to Germany, because none of the powers which took part in the Munich Conference had given the promised guarantees for the nation – a nation that in any case had already been mortally amputated and lay at Germany's mercy. And yet it was this very occupation of Prague by Hitler that led to a turning point in statesmanship and in history. For now Hitler himself had conspicuously violated the principle of the right of the self-determination of peoples, the principle that up to now he had made the cardinal tenet of his own policy. The world's opinion once and for all realized that Hitler was interested in more than a reasonable policy of revision. Realization dawned that the man did not stand by his word; did not feel bound by treaties; and looked at negotiations only as means of exerting pressure, or of manufacturing alibis to present to history. Hitler had started running amok in Europe. His foreign policy was without precedent in its continuing violations of the traditions of European politics: traditions that recognized the application of force as a last resort – but never as the starting point of statecraft.

The same English Government that up to now had considered Hitler's arguments as being weighty enough to justify a European policy of concessions to the Führer now took an opposite tack. Great Britain began building a policy of firmness. She recognized that so unreliable a politician as Hitler had unforeseeable ambitions; and in order to set limits to them, Great Britain decided no longer to shrink from the danger of war. Incidentally, the occupation of Prague was experienced even by many National Socialists as a disappointment, a political rupture – somewhat as the events of June 30, 1934, had struck them. They saw that Hitler was now taking leave of the principle of German nationhood; it had been a guiding star to many of his adherents and had helped them to preserve easy consciences despite their leader's dubious political methods.

As for the English, their experiences with Hitler's foreign policy in the years from 1935 to 1939 helps to account for the uncompromising determination with which they pursued the war under the doctrine of unconditional surrender. The demand for unconditional surrender was understandable in view of Hitler's incapacity for real understanding and honest co-operation; this was so even though after 1945 there was many an occasion on which to regret the promulgation of the doctrine.

Another reason for this uncompromising attitude was grounded in what was going on inside Germany. Events there were shaping up as such an offense to the tenets of human civilization that the events could no longer be shrugged off by other nations as an internal affair of the Reich. The National Socialist policy of anti-Semitism and the persecution of the Jews in the Third Reich stemmed from motives that lay deeper than all merely political considerations of good and bad. What went on was beyond the pale of man's normal relationships with man.

The unique quality of the National Socialist persecution of the Jews was that it led to a systematic, assembly-line scheme for destruction. This action cannot be explained simply by reference to traditional anti-Semitism. Instead, its real root is in an ideological development of that epoch: Biological-materialistic concepts invaded the realm of political thinking. In the decade of the nineties in the past century, a number of theorists based their views of human history and of social and political arrangements on Darwin's hypotheses in natural science – and they made corresponding suggestions for reform. These so-called "social Darwinists", scholars such as Wilhelm Schallmeyer, Alfred Ploetz, Otto Ammon and Alexander Tille, had rightly recognized that human destiny and political life are both biologically conditioned to a certain degree. But they built their findings into an inadmissible generalization: They concluded that biological conditions were the ultimately decisive factors – and that, moreover, these factors were available to control by human beings. They believed that to a certain extent the human being could become the breeder of himself and of his kind. This social-Darwinistic theory of the breeding of human stock made a lasting impression on some of the leading National Socialists, and it played a major role in both their ideology and their practice. The fatal error in this theory is that it involves granting to some human beings the power of disposition over their kind – a concept that *a priori* is incompatible with a belief in the freedom and dignity of the human condition. For between the breeder and those to be bred there can develop no human communication such as that which links individuals who in principle are equals. Far from it; those to be bred are depreciated to the role of expendible objects, a prey to biological interference and manipulation. The relation between breeder and bred is without any personal content. For this reason, it need not even lead to inhuman practices, in the conventional meaning of "inhuman" (as, for example, the extirpation of all individuals considered to be inferior), in order to be considered devoid of humanity. The doctrine is already inhuman if it contemplates a purposeful breeding of those individuals who are considered valuable.

National Socialists looked on their own people, and during the second World War on the people of Europe, as plantations that have been irrationally laid out and where weeds are growing lushly. What such plantations needed, in National Socialist eyes, was to be reduced to order. And order was to be created by isolating the "asocial types", eliminating the "ferments of decomposition", building up the "valuable" elements, and getting rid of "inferior" stock: by sterilizing the ill, by transplanting or "weeding out" national or ethnic groups that were "trouble-makers". In the end, there was to have been a new European society, rationally and biologically planned. The most horrible of the National Socialist crimes were part of this insane effort to reform political life by breeding and selection – and thus neatly to rearrange Europe. Tools for this purpose included euthanasia, sterilization, re-settlement, "Germanization", and the eradication of whole categories of human beings that were looked upon as worthless or dangerous.

These ideologists stripped Jews of human attributes. A Jew was less than an enemy that one fights; less than the hated fellow-man with whom one shares the common traits of humanity even if one murders him. The Jew, rather, was considered a virus in the body of the state, a pest that had to be destroyed. That is why the persecution of the Jews resembled a campaign against a pest – a kind of act of disinfection that lacked any human concern for the victims.

The sponsors of this wholesale action and those who carried it out were not affected in the least as fellow-creatures with their victims – or at least did not want to be so affected. But by their own logic they conceivably deprived themselves of a claim to be considered as fellow-humans. For when dealing with individuals who were capable of denying the status of human being to others, one could hardly conclude an armistice and a peace treaty; rather, such individuals had to be brought to unconditional surrender. True, the unconditional surrender was levied on the German people as a whole. But that is simply the reverse side of a tragic entanglement: The initiator of the inhumanity not only belonged to this people, but he had also been successful in contending that his will was to be identified with the will of his people.

The biological annihilation of the Jews was prepared for by the continuing worsening of their status in society. At the same time, a gradual change in the political climate was brought about, and a resultant narcotization of the population in its concern for the Jewish fate. The Jewish policy of the first years of the Third Reich had to steer a cautious course between radical tendencies and enforced circumspection. While there was no limit on the propaganda of hate, the "official" elimination of the Jews from public life was pursued in those years under a mantle of comparative "correctness". By 1935, the possibilities of a persecution based on at least sketchy legal underpinnings was exhausted. In that year, the "Nuremberg Laws" prepared the way for the isolation of the Jews from society.

The next major step became possible only in connection with the acts of 1938 that began turning normal life upside-down. A few weeks after the Munich Conference had saved peace once again, a German counselor of legation in Paris, vom Rath, was murdered by a Jew. This event was made the ground for the pogrom of November 8 and 9, 1938. It was followed by a hail of laws and regulations which made the Jews dependent upon an overlordship that was their sworn enemy. In particular, they were pushed out of the country's economic life. In normal times the business world had been relatively independent of politics, and the removal of the Jews would have been rather difficult. But by now the Jews had been reduced to so low a status, and had been so far removed from the public eye, that their final disappearance could no longer cause any great sensation. The planned killing began during the campaign against Russia; and eventually it became organized, with the rational planning of an industry. This effort created the notorious extermination camps in the East. Thus an idea was realized that Hitler had expressed back in 1924, when he wrote in "Mein Kampf" (p. 772, German edition): "If at the beginning of the war, and during it, 12,000 or 15,000 of these Hebrew corrupters of the people could have been held under poison gas, as hundreds of thousands of our best German manpower from all levels and callings had to suffer it at the front, then the million-fold sacrifice on the battlefields would not have been in vain. On the contrary: 12,000 scoundrels removed at the right time might well have saved the lives of a million decent Germans for our future."

45

After the annexation of Czechoslovakia, there was not even a brief pause that might have enabled Europe to nourish the illusion that Hitler's demands were now satisfied. Instead the Fuehrer turned his attention in the direction of Poland. On March 21, 1939, he conveyed to the Polish Ambassador in Berlin some suggestions for the solution of problems concerning Danzig and the Corridor. The Polish Government did not go along with his original intention of making Poland a satellite, as part of his *Lebensraum-*policy directed against Russia. Moreover, Great Britain's reaction this time was unequivocal. On March 31, Chamberlain, speaking for both his own and the French Government, issued a declaration guaranteeing the integrity of Poland. This guarantee, it is true, expressly mentioned that Germany still had legitimate grounds to seek a revision of the German-Polish situation; but Chamberlain also said that none of the outstanding questions justified substitution of the use of force for peaceful negotiation. Hitler's reply was to give notice of withdrawal from the German-British naval agreement of 1935, as well as from his 1934 pact with Poland; and also to conclude a military alliance with Italy.

As the rival constellations of powers closed ranks, both sides strove for the favor of the Soviet Union. Britain and France had already ob-

46

tained a preliminary agreement with Moscow, after overcoming considerable diplomatic obstacles. But then the Russians demanded the right of marching through Poland and Rumania – something that the West could not bring itself to concede. There were no such scruples on the German side. Accordingly, Ribbentrop was able to sign a German-Soviet non-aggression pact in the Kremlin on August 23. In a secret annex, the pact recognized Finland, Latvia, Esthonia, Bessarabia and the eastern part of Poland as being within the Soviet sphere of interest. All this only to enable Hitler to advance his tactics against Poland. In doing so, Hitler, the supposed "European bulwark against Bolshevism", obviously was not hesitating to throw overboard an essential part of his purported ideology. At the same time, his deal with the Soviet Union sacrificed not only the interests of Europe in general but also, in the long range, those of Germany. At the same time that he handed over some small European states and ethnic groups to the political arbitration of Moscow, which was an act grave enough in itself, he destroyed the protective or buffer zone that they had formed. And thus he cleared the Soviet Union's road into Europe.

What Hitler was after was a free hand in the East, unmolested by Western European powers. Now, as a counterpart to his policy in favor of pacts involving only two nations, he leaned toward the prosecution of wars involving only two nations. His problem was not whether he could avoid a war with Poland, but whether he could keep England – and thereby France as well – out of it. But if he hoped to attain this state of affairs by his arrangement with Moscow, he was to be disappointed: On August 25, England confirmed her new course by announcing conclusion of a formal mutual-assistance pact with Poland. On the same day, Mussolini let it be known that Italy was not ready for war. Under the impact of this news, Hitler revoked his order for an attack on Poland, already scheduled to take place on the next day, August 26. He entered into new negotiations with Great Britain. The British Government indicated that it was ready to use any last chance to save the peace – in contrast to the Polish Government, which, overestimating Polish strength, failed to exert the utmost effort to avoid a contest of arms. But England did not agree to the "understanding" that Hitler proposed at Poland's expense and, in its ultimate effect, at the expense of Europe as well. So it was that Hitler launched his attack on Poland on September 1, still acting in the belief that the Western powers, if he could only present them with a fait accompli, once more would put up with one.

After the series of victorious "lightning wars" – the *Blitzkriege* – against Poland, Denmark and Norway, Belgium, Holland and France, Hitler was at the apex, not of his power, it is true, but of his triumphs and his unclouded successes. By now the consequences of Versailles had been erased, and the humiliation of the surrender of 1918 had been extinguished by a brilliant campaign. The German nation seemed to have attained a new pinnacle in its history.

* * *

At this point it is highly significant to understand something that was going on inside Germany at a time during which there was no hint of a German collapse from external forces. Clear symptoms were beginning to appear of a change from within: a sort of disintegration of structure of the state, and a dissolution of the classical line of "national" thinking. A new tendency was gathering momentum, and it veered away from the "national principles" that heretofore had been the unquestioned foundation of politics. This change came about partly under the influence of Hitler's anarchic attitude toward politics and statesmanship; for, in spite of all his Prussian-sounding phrases, he lacked any real sense of the nature of the state. And the change

49

also came about partly as a consequence of the National Socialist ideology itself. But finally, and this is perhaps most significant for observers today, the crumbling of "nationalist" foundations inside Germany was caused by some far-reaching eddies and currents of our time, which are as strong today as they were then, and which even the most determined political program cannot withstand of itself.

The story of this dissolution of "nationalism" inside Germany at the height of the Hitler "national" dictatorship begins with the claims put forward by the National Socialists. The party pretended that it alone represented the political will of the German people. Moreover, it claimed to derive its authority in no wise from the concept of the state, but from forces within the party itself. This approach alone reduced the authority of the state to a sometime thing. It promptly became an open question whether state or party was on top. Originally, the NSDAP conceived of its relationship to the state in this way: The party would have the political initiative, and the state would have the task of implementing the broad outlines of policy laid down by the party. This concept soon collapsed. It ran up against the nature of the bureaucracy. For the traditional apparatus of the German state was more than the National Socialists had bargained for. The bureaucracy, it became clear, was not merely an apparatus that obediently carried out any and all orders from the top. It was a stable and well-organized machinery of administration – a kind of law unto itself in that it had rules and procedures for governing, down to the smallest details. This very independence of the German bureaucracy was, under the National Socialists, its undoing. The more the party opened its eyes to the self-sufficiency of the governmental apparatus, the more power the NSDAP began taking over. In the course of time, the party assumed for itself not only the major policy-making decisions, but also functions that had formerly belonged exclusively to the realm of the permanent civil service and of the state. The party took over these powers by forming executive agencies outside the governmental apparatus. From the start, these new organizations were geared not to the German government as such, but to Hitler's political plans and methods.

By far the best example of this rearrangement of power within – and outside – the state was the *Schutz-Staffel*, the SS. From its general staff it developed a new bureaucracy. This SS state-within-a-state (or more correctly, state-outside-a-state), took over more and more rights and functions of the traditional German apparatus of government. The significance of this new distribution of power is expressed in a letter by the chief of the SS office for "racial and resettlement" questions, from the spring of 1939. It states: "In my opinion, the problem of resettlement, especially beyond the borders of the old Reich, is first and foremost political. It follows that the disposition of these matters should be assigned to a political organization – that is, to the SS. It should take over these responsibilities; they should not be left to the ministerial offices. The latter up to now have distinguished themselves as being unsuited for carrying out political assignments."

The first and also most outstanding "political assignment" to be taken over by the SS was within the realm of police power; and the most striking aspect of that transfer was the rise of the SS political police. The position of »Chief of the German Police« was created in the summer of 1936. The new job was linked to the office of the SS *Reichsführer*. So it came about that the Reich Minister of the Interior lost, not only de facto but de jure as well, his former sovereignty over the police. The change had the effect of unifying and nationalizing the police – but nationalizing them under an ever more extra-national authority, the SS. Moreover, the transfer of police powers was the first in a series of changes that gradually abolished the competencies of the

Minister of the Interior in favor of the SS. Further stages were the creation of the Reich Central Security Office, and the appointment of the SS *Reichsführer* as "Reich commissioner for the consolidation of German nationhood". The climax came in the summer of 1943, when the Reich Ministry of the Interior itself was taken over by the SS *Reichsführer*.

Yet it was not only that groups created by the party – such as the SS – were taking over traditional functions of government. The mere process by which Hitler tightened his grip as Führer transformed the nature of the government over the years. As early as the last pre-war years, Hitler was represented as the sole representative of the people's will. In other words, his person was supposed to have become the real source and expression of sovereignty. From Hitler, under this concept, stemmed any and all sovereign power in state and party. His task was no longer to rule within a framework of laws, but rather to exercise his political will in any way that seemed suitable to him. In enforcing his rule, he made the state administration one of his instruments of power. And the state administration was no longer to derive its legitimacy from law, but rather from the political will of the leadership.

Here is a characteristic technique that this absolutist form of rulership used to consolidate its power: The Führer would inform a regular administrative agency of the government that it was no longer responsible for this or that function; instead, the function was being taken over by a special deputy. The deputy, of course, was subordinate and directly responsible only to the Führer. The use of this technique created a new structure that, administratively and legally, amounted to martial law. It is no wonder that in due time the super-structure's conflicts with the traditional government led to an immense chaos of overlapping competences – of functions that duplicated and cancelled each other. The dictatorship's administrative technique carried a considerable price tag. In the last years of the war, particularly, Hitler's method of getting his individual wishes carried out began backfiring. He had cut corners by detouring around the usual administrative channels. But by doing so, he had thrown monkey-wrenches into an apparatus which had been engineered to serve the long-range interests of the nation. Just when he was about to need the efficiency of the German machinery of state, Hitler was recklessly going about dismantling the whole apparatus. Constantly he ordered the establishment of new agencies of power, without, however, allowing time for them to achieve smooth operating efficiency. Every time he took a new initiative, he ended up canceling or at least blunting it by issuing a demand in furtherance of some new effort. Wherever a new body of law might have established itself, it was soon short-circuited for the sake of some new purpose of the day. The result was increased confusion. Far from moving toward a subtly rationalized, carefully co-ordinated mechanism of government, the National Socialist state lurched into a dictated chaos. The exercise of power under Hitler became organized confusion. Disorder increased as the dictator moved with relentless consistency toward "total" goals, goals that sacrificed both state and people.

The end of World War I had brought fargoing changes in German attitudes toward nationalism. First of all, the monarchy which had stood for national feeling was replaced by a democratic constitution. From the outset, many persons and groups denied that the new set-up had a chance of giving worthy and successful representation to German interests. The problem was in part psychological: National pride – which shrunk from acknowledging military defeat, which wanted to prove its unbroken will to fight, which was unable for the time being to get anywhere against the enemies of war days – found an outlet in a new direction. It turned against the existing form of government. Such national pride assumed that the overthrow of the democratic order would be the essential first step toward achieving a national resurgence. This brand of nationalism, whose devotees assumed that their attitudes had no chance at all of gaining ascendancy under the democratic order, underwent a process of sublimation. This transformation, this idealizing of nationalism, represented anything but a purging of the minds of those who were dedicated to it. Their nationalistic ardor went underground – only to smoulder. This suppressed political drive changed from a plan for political activity into an attitude, a way of thinking, a way of life. The temporary sublimation or suppression of the urge to achieve national pride was experienced by its devotees as a kind of withdrawal: a withdrawal into a concept of a nation that somehow was immune to any external defeat. This changed kind of nationalism took on the generalized nature and the absolutism of a moral imperative. Some even found that for them it could become a substitute for religion.

To this suppressed nationalistic urge were added new components as our century brought technological and social changes. A mixture of new ideas helped to form the National Socialist ethos. For example, a dream was dreamed of the total worker-state. Another dream was dreamed of a state based on new theories of natural selection. From these components, blended with suppressed nationalism, evolved the manifold formulas of the national-revolutionary urge of the 1920s. Those who felt this new urge distanced themselves from the old pre-war political and social order quite as ardently as they fought against the Weimar Republic. Eventually these various currents of national-revolutionary urges merged into National Socialism. Then, after it came to power, something unexpected happened. The revolutionary components of the National Socialist urge burst out of the confines of nationhood and nationalism. As a result, the history of the Third Reich offers the strange spectacle of an extremely nationalistic regime that ended up by destroying the national idea.

This destruction of German national unity by forces that were considered nationalist can be traced to a very tangible beginning. The whole development stemmed from the existence of a party that did two related things: First, it made out that its own will was nothing less or more than the will of the nation. Secondly, it demanded that the status it claimed for itself receive official recognition and universal obedience. In other words, the party maintained that agreement with its views was dedication to the nation, and that disagreement was treason. The doctrine began by forcing many persons who had been "nationally oriented" into a conflict of conscience—and ended up by splitting asunder the entire German community. The National Socialists branded whole groups of Germans as enemies of the NSDAP way of life—as Germans with whom party leaders felt no more oneness than with nations against which the party pursued its war. "This war is a war of a way of life", stated an oft-quoted party slogan. The slogan equated the inner front—all Germans who rejected National Socialism – with the outer fronts. And this inner front ran right across the nation. Another non-German aspect was that the National Socialists within Germany felt closer ties with National Socialists outside Germany than with non-National Socialists within the nation's borders.

There is one especially clear symptom of this departure from the framework of traditional "national" thinking. It became evident after the end of the military campaign in France. The party began building up the "Germanic SS" – a no-longer-German, but rather an international body. Within the new international SS, members of other European nations received the same privileges as German soldiers – if they declared themselves to be National Socialists, or at least to be foes of Bolshevism; and provided they met certain racial requirements set up by the SS.

Doubtless one could have found within these units, built up and led by a small clique of strongly ideological individuals, some kernels of European thinking. But these nuclei were soon snuffed out, sacrificed to the requirements of the day. The truth is that the top National Socialist leadership was far from possessing a positive concept of a European policy; rather it regarded the populations within its sphere of power merely as subject nationalities, to be more or less frankly exploited – even, if need be, as cannon fodder on the Russian front.

The racist-biological theories that seemed in the beginning to be an extreme version of "national" thinking soon turned out to be the very antithesis of nationalism. We have seen that the NSDAP political ideology divided the nation. An even sharper line of cleavage was cut across Germany by the racist philosophy of the NSDAP leadership. This cleavage becomes clearest, of course, in the persecution of the Jews – a persecution that victimized many individuals who placed Germany first in their hearts. The fact that one was racially a Jew weighed more heavily in the scales than the fact that one was nationally, culturally and avowedly a German. Just how definitely this materialist-biological ideology gradually superseded political and national considerations can be observed in the treatment of Jewish front-fighters of World War I. At first these Jewish war heroes were exempted from certain measures of persecution under the Third Reich, on grounds of their "national" merits. Later, however, they were treated exactly like other Jews. If one of them dared during the Second World War to put on his old military decorations, this was considered an "impertinent Jewish provocation".

Then there was another enormous deed of violence against genuinely national interests. It too had historic import: namely, the action that took place around the year 1939 to re-settle Germans from the South Tyrol, Esthonia, Latvia, Volhynia, Bessarabia, Bukovina and Dobrudja. Recklessly the National Socialists sacrificed to their purposes of the day centuries-old centers of German culture and influence: whether in the South Tyrol in order to make sure of Mussolini's good will, or in the Eastern territories in order to grant Soviet Russia a sphere of influence, for the sake of buying Soviet toleration of the war against Poland. It was with a view to gaining short-term advantages that the liquidation of German culture and influence – of the so-called *Deutschtum* – was undertaken in Eastern Europe. Then the Russians completed the liquidation. What is one to say of this goal of supposedly "national" German policy, this object of concentrating the whole German people within the borders of Germany? It was of course a dilettante idea. And it made no sense if judged in the light of the declared National Socialist policy of winning extra territory – *Lebensraum* – for Germany. More remarkable, however, than the fact that the NSDAP worked against its own goals is the fact that still another short-range motive initiated a resettlement campaign even before the war, even before the pact with the Soviet Union.

The motive behind this earlier mass operation to bring people within the jurisdiction of the Reich was revealed at the beginning of 1939. It was outlined in a speech by the organizer of the resettlement, SS Chief Group Leader Greifelt. He spoke in his capacity as the SS Reichsführer's deputy for matters connected with Hitler's Four Years Plan. Greifelt had the job of procuring the "human material" needed for the policy of autonomy that was initiated in 1936. Greifelt said: Germany already was short of manpower. She would feel the pinch even more if there were a military mobilization. Nor could this shortage be alleviated by hiring foreign workers, he continued: Germany was also short of foreign exchange. Then he explained a way out of the dilemma. Beyond Germany's borders, there were 30,000,000 German citizens and "ethnic Germans" – and at the moment they were putting their energy and skill at the disposal of foreign nations. Here, said Greifelt, were the natural reserves that could be used to supply the Reich with the extra workers it needed. At that time the Führer, he developed, had already ordered the SS Reichsführer to start the resettlement action. – In plain terms, the regime needed extra working power to man its war-geared economy. The National Socialists considered this need a sufficient justification for taking a step fraught with drastic potentialities for Germany's future: The regime set out to liquidate age-old communities of German-speaking ethnic groups living beyond the Reich's borders.

In spite of such non-national (so far as true national interests were concerned) actions, it is self-evident that National Socialism did, in fact, also retain some extremely nationalistic traits until the last. But behind its national façade, as we have already noted, the regime concealed forces that operated quite otherwise. These hidden forces ended up by destroying the old foundations of national-political thinking. Meanwhile, they also corroded the fabric of the community and the nation. Much more still than that, these new forces operated to involve Germany in guilt of the first order.

This then is the point of our story of the Third Reich's destruction of traditional governmental and political frameworks: It would be utterly unrealistic for even the warmest friend of Germany to attempt to defend, or to apologize for, the Third Reich, by urging that it served "nationalist" needs. And there is a corollary point that emerges from our story: It would be equally unrealistic for anybody to see in the experience of the years of the Third Reich a justification of the old, pre-Hitler "national" attitudes. On the contrary, the course taken by the Third Reich proves that "nationalism" simply can no longer cope with the perils peculiar to our time.

These dangers of our era once assumed the particular guise of National Socialism. But the perils have outlasted the National Socialists; they continue to take on ever more serious import for peoples all over the globe. Among the present-day forms of these dangers are ideological dogmatism; a scorn for justice and law; unalloyed materialism; and the dictatorship of purposes – that old, still living idea that the end justifies any means. The most striking proof we have that nationalism is outdated is this: A regime that was born under the star of "national revival" gradually destroyed true nationalism and then destroyed the nation itself. There is a clear moral for us in the National Socialist years: We must learn no longer to consider the nation in itself as an absolute value. For that reason, political arguments based on purely national grounds can no longer claim to be the fount of all political wisdom. Nothing in the recent history that we are reviewing here forces the conclusion that people are no longer to love their country. Yet the German experience has shown that a people which loves his fellow-countrymen and his nationhood must be prepared to let national absolutism wither away. We need new, non-nationalistic political concepts if we want to avoid such dangers as have already been exemplified for us all in the terrible course and climax of the experiment called National Socialism.

* * *

Hitler had led the campaign against France in the summer of 1940 in the certainty that its conclusion would bring about peace in the West, and a free hand in the East. For he had no doubt that, after France's defeat, Great Britain at last would be ready for a compromise. There is an evidence of Hitler's expectations in the relatively mild armistice conditions that he decreed for France – one of the rare instances in which Hitler showed moderation. This relative mildness may be taken as proof that his one and only intention in the West was to get out of his military engagements there in order to be able to turn toward the goals that he considered foremost. Even while the campaign in the West was still going on, he told Jodl that he was determined to settle accounts with the Soviet Union, as soon as the military situation would let him. So it was a cause of great chagrin to him – a disappointment that he could not swallow for a long time – when England did not soften its attitude. On the contrary, the British made their intentions clear by their attack on the French fleet near Oran on July 3, 1940. They were not disposed to hand Hitler a peace now that he had started a war. On the other hand, to force Great Britain to make peace shaped up as a highly difficult task – and a military risk that Hitler evaded. Although it is true that he ordered preparations for an attack on the British Isles, he was actually only half-hearted about the idea. In fact, he took pains to stress – not at all in accord with his usual approach – the considerable technical and military difficulties of the operation.

When it became apparent in September 1940 that the invasion would no longer be possible during that year, Hitler made efforts on the diplomatic front to merge his actual and potential allies in making common cause against England. On October 23 he met with Franco in Hendaye and tried to induce him to enter the war and to join in an attack on Gibraltar; but Franco was evasive. Next day, Hitler tried in Montoire to win over Pétain for France's active participation in the battle against England. But the two reached only a general agreement, a plan for co-operation – of which Pétain said later that it would take six months to work it out and other six months to forget it again. Finally, during the first months of 1941, Hitler tried to interest Japan in a struggle with the British Empire, and specifically in an attack on Singapore; also without success. Where Hitler had no opportunity of applying the threat of force, his diplomacy failed. So it was that he failed in his diplomatic manoeuvres to mount an attack on key positions of Britain's world empire as he failed in his military preparations for the occupation of the British Isles.

In the meantime, developments in Eastern Europe were giving Hitler serious grounds for concern. While he was directing the campaign in France, the Soviets on June 16 had occupied Esthonia and Latvia, as well as (contrary to the secret annex to the agreement of August 23, 1939) Lithuania. On June 26 the Soviet Union forced Rumania to relinquish not only Bessarabia which Hitler's Reich had awarded to the U.S.S.R. in the secret annex, but North Bukovina as well. The resultant turmoil in the Balkans (Hungary and Bulgaria also put in claims) Hitler tried to settle by the so-called Second Arbitration of Vienna on August 30. The latter event, however, was interpreted by the U.S.S.R. as a German act of interference in Russia's Balkan policy. As such, Moscow felt, it was no more in keeping with the spirit of the German-Soviet non-aggression pact than was the "Tripartite Pact" that was concluded by Germany, Italy and Japan (the anti-Comintern powers!) on September 27 – even though it was true that the pact, in this case, was to foster the formation of a common front against England.

The critical situation in the Balkans was intensified when Mussolini marched from Albania into Greece on October 28. By doing so, the Duce risked not only military intervention by England – something Hitler particularly feared – but also Russian intervention. Hitler, accordingly, felt forced to secure the Balkans by the campaign against Yugoslavia and Greece in the spring of 1941. Hitler's invitation to the Soviet Foreign Minister to come to Berlin which Molotov accepted with his visit from November 12 to 14, 1940, was intended to try to divert the Soviet Union's inconvenient interest in Eastern Europe to the south of the Asian continent. In a conference that took place in an air-raid shelter, Ribbentrop sought to persuade Molotov that Great Britain was already as good as defeated, and that it only remained for the British to grasp that fact. Molotov replied: "If that is true, why are we in this shelter, and whose bombs are those that are falling outside?" He refused to discuss which parts of the allegedly disintegrating British Empire the German regime had assigned to the Soviet Union, and insisted instead on discussing the concrete problems outstanding between Berlin and Moscow.

As for the shining military successes that Hitler had achieved up to now, they had not contributed in the slightest degree to the solution of the two great problems with which he had saddled himself in order to have his way against Poland: the war in the West, and the uncertain alliance in the East. The danger of a war on two fronts was not banished by the pact with the Soviet Union, but was only postponed. In order momentarily to win over the U.S.S.R. to his side in the summer of 1939, Hitler had conceded to the Russians positions that, in the very next year, were considerably to curtail his freedom of action. The Russians had approached so near that at any moment they could create very serious difficulties, purely by diplomatic means and without needing to resort to military undertakings. On the other side, it was becoming clear that England lay outside the sphere within which the success of an attack depended upon nothing else than the accomplishments of the German armed forces.

In this dilemma – East or West? – Hitler tipped the scales in favor of a campaign against the Soviet Union. In an attack on the United Kingdom, he would have risked the loss of his military prestige in any case: For whether he had launched his forces against the home islands themselves, or had committed them instead – in a potential campaign for which the auspices were good – against the British positions in the Eastern Mediterranean, in either event he would have had to plunge into the unfamiliar sphere of naval warfare. An attack in the East, on the other hand, could be mounted in the style that his armed forces already had proved in action; and Hitler had no doubt that he could defeat the Soviet Union before Great Britain would be in a position to retaliate by, for example, daring an invasion of the Continent. Once Hitler had triumphed over the Soviet Union, it appeared to him that he would have eliminated the danger of an alliance between the Russians and the British. Moreover, Germany would then have control of the mineral resources of the East – and with them at her disposal, she would not need to fear any contest with England, no matter how difficult. Finally, the "Lebensraum" that Hitler sought, the extra land whose conquest had been the target of Germany's policy since 1936, was located in the East. Then why make a difficult detour via England, when the real goal could be attained much more easily?

It was such considerations that led to the fatal

decision of attacking the Soviet Union. The plain fact was that the enterprise that stretched ahead of Hitler was unfathomable, especially as he even lacked the means to cope with his already existing – and not simpler – military problems. One has the impression that Hitler very likely had no clear notion of the breadth of either the British or the Soviet empire, but only grasped the extent of the areas that immediately impinged on continental Europe.

When the attack on the Soviet Union had already been decided upon, Rudolf Hess, Hitler's deputy and loyal follower, flew to England under adventurous circumstances. There he tried on his own initiative and by his personal intervention to obtain for Hitler, at the eleventh hour, his much-wished-for peace in the West. While the Hess enterprise was completely unimportant as far as foreign policy was concerned, it did have, however, the most serious effect on the domestic political situation in Germany. For it opened the way to power for Martin Bormann. Under Bormann's influence, all the seeds of harm inherent both in the absolutist doctrine of the Führer and in the materialist ideology of National Socialism developed and attained full growth. Hitler did away with the office of "Deputy to the Führer", and appointed Bormann chief of the party secretariat; later, "Secretary to the Führer".

With this title, Bormann soon took up auto-
cratic powers in the ante-room of power. For
all party and state affairs that were to go to Hitler for decision had to be channeled through Bormann. Meanwhile, however, Hitler was turning
his interest almost exclusively to the military
leadership, and wanted to avoid as far as he could
getting entangled in other matters. So the command of Germany's internal affairs fell, to all
intents and purposes, into the lap of Martin Bormann. He could determine who was permitted to
speak to Hitler. He could decide which matters
got through to Hitler – and with what sort of
commentary attached to them – for decision. At
the same time, Bormann, acting in the name of
the Führer, could intervene whenever he pleas-
ed in any issue, whether party or governmental.
The more Hitler came to distrust his bureaucracy
and the leadership of the armed forces, the more
he tended to transfer the implementation of the
war effort to the organization that he felt he could
trust to be loyal and to make the impossible
possible: his National Socialist party. One of his
most important moves in this direction was to
name his NSDAP Gauleiters as Reich defense
commissioners, a step taken in the autumn of
1942.

The resultant political activization of the party
led to increasing tension between NSDAP and

SS. Up to then, the SS had enjoyed more or less unchallenged control of the extra-governmental executive power, particularly at the top level of the Reich administration. Meanwhile the party had occupied itself with regional administrative affairs, from the level of the Gau downward. Now, the more the party, under Bormann's leadership, moved in upon the Reich administration, the more the SS began to extend its own sphere of interest to regional affairs. This move by the SS was especially noticeable after Himmler became minister of the interior in 1943. The debate finally revolved around whether stronger powers should be conferred upon the administrative office of Landrat, as Himmler wanted, or upon the party office of Kreisleiter, as Bormann demanded. Not that the matter in question was any longer the integrity of state authorities as such. Rather, the quarrel had degenerated into a tug-o'-war between the two most powerful National Socialist organizations. Although the SS had gained a definite edge in actual power during the years 1935 to 1940, nevertheless the party was able to catch up to a considerable degree during the later stages of the war. And this was so because Bormann had far greater influence with Hitler than Himmler did. Nevertheless, the SS remained the stronger of the two organizations, and the one with a more marked political profile.

In fact, under a politically more self-sufficient leader than Himmler, the SS would have been able to eliminate the party at any time.

Bormann had been chief of the party secretariat for not quite a month when, at the beginning of June 1941, he addressed a circular to all Gauleiter on the basic incompatibility of National Socialist and Christian views. This incompatibility the churches had discovered themselves as early as 1933, when the party was still claiming to be rooted in a "positive Christianity". Realizing the true state of affairs, the church had refused to go along with the efforts at "co-ordination". Since this initial failure, Hitler had tried gradually to suffocate the churches with a policy of creeping terror. A first stage came after the reincorporation of the Saar into the Reich in 1935. At that point, the propaganda machinery began demanding the so-called "de-confessionalization of public life". This move allegedly was directed only against unjustifiable interference by the churches in political affairs. But the real aim was to deprive the churches of their influence on worldly matters in general. As the party philosopher Rosenberg once expressed it in his "Messages on the Philosophical Situation": "The earth on which we live is absolutely no concern of the churches any longer."

This was only the first stage, this "de-confessionalization" with its fiction that the world of faith was still being recognized as a sphere of its own, co-existing with the political sphere. The pretense was dropped in the early part of 1938. The minister for church affairs, Kerrl, announced the slogan for the next stage of the campaign against the churches: "Religion and philosophy of life are identical." Shortly afterward, the foreign-policy concerns of the years 1938 and 1939, and then the onset of war, temporarily decreased the intensity of the anti-church campaign. In 1941, however, Bormann extracted the practical conclusions from Kerrl's sentence by writing one of his own: "All influences that could infringe upon the leadership of the nation, as exercised by the Führer with the help of the NSDAP, must be eliminated. To an ever-increasing degree the people must be extricated from the churches and from their executives, the clergy."

In a similar vein, Hitler himself had already emphasized on various occasions that the churches could not share in the leadership of the people, inasmuch as the churches, like the National Socialist movement, claimed the whole man. Thus in the Third Reich the basic antagonism in the field of religion was not the conflict between church and state (a classic problem of national policy), but rather a conflict between the church and a party ideology. It was a case of

74

two competing institutions with the same sort of claim on their adherents.

That is to say, the NSDAP sought to be more than a mere political institution, with political aims. It wanted to renew Germany by means of "a new faith", a "political faith" – and the word "faith" by no means was to be taken only figuratively. Hitler had sensed the religious perplexity and the unarticulated longings of his generation. He went about creating a substitute for religious faith – and sought to evoke a surge of faith that would serve his political goals. In accord with this goal, he demanded for his movement a monopoly not only of the nation's political leadership but also of the moral and ethical leadership. In the last analysis, the matter at issue in the so-called *Kirchenkampf* or struggle with the church was not the repudiation of this or that clerical prerogative. The issue was not simply the disavowal of this or that Christian dogma. What was involved for Hitler and his party was nothing less than the spiritual and ethical loyalty of the individual human being. A party of *Weltanschauung* cannot tolerate the idea that human beings might act from other motives and according to other standards than those of the party's own world-encompassing ideology. Therefore such a party's rule is not simply a political, but a totalitarian, tyranny. Such a party does not limit its efforts to the complete control of the apparatus of government or even to the complete control of the external affairs of those whom it rules. It also claims power over the conscience. A totalitarian state tolerates no expressions of conscience – of whatever sort – which might involve the possibility that an individual at some point could distance himself from the purposes of the organized whole. Far from it: A totalitarian state confronts the individual with a basic dilemma. Either he goes along unconditionally with the pattern of state power (and thereby abandons himself) or he remains true to himself (and thereby invites his own destruction). By setting up such totalitarian patterns, the Third Reich abandoned the standards of national political thought. It abandoned a normal political frame of reference altogether. It impinged upon – indeed, challenged – the spiritual existence of the human personality.

It is this aspect, by the way, that clarifies the fundamental difference between National Socialism on the one hand and the fascist regimes in Italy and Spain on the other. The latter regimes made less comprehensive claims of supremacy. They did not usurp the functions of the churches, but instead were content to remain within the traditional frame of reference of a political organization that makes a claim to leadership. For that reason, fascism as such could never endanger the political substructure of the state and the substance of the nation – or alter the conditions of life of the individual – as fundamentally and as insupportably as did the totalitarian regime in Germany. On the other hand, the close relationship between National Socialism and Bolshevism is obvious at once. One recognizes the guile in the National Socialists' claim that they were defending Europe against the Bolshevist peril, and one can understand, in this respect, the uncompromising pertinacity with which Great Britain and the United States fought Hitler's Germany. For the same danger that Europe previously had had to fear in the form of Bolshevism had now suddenly burst into view in the heart of the Continent – threatening Europe from the inside. What National Socialism may have lacked in a certain primitive spirit of barbarism was made up for by the frightening continuity of the attempt to pervert the European spirit. In recognition of this fact, an opposition sprang up within Germany. The opposition rejected National Socialism on ethical and spiritual grounds, regardless of the successes or failures the NSDAP might be encountering. Dietrich Bonhoeffer, a representative of the resistance, once said: "Hitler is the Anti-Christ. We must accordingly proceed with our work and eradicate him, no matter whether he is successful or no." This sentence can be understood only if one has perceived that, while claiming to speak for the nation, the Third Reich was actually setting in motion forces that attacked the roots of human existence, and therefore also attacked the nation, along with every other entity that finds its roots in humanity.

After Hitler had defeated Yugoslavia and Greece in a quick campaign in April 1941, he launched the war against the Soviet Union on June 22. At the start it brought him the greatest imaginable series of triumphs. But the Führer's confident intention of winding up the war by the onset of winter was not fulfilled. On the contrary, the German advance ground to a halt at the very gates of Moscow on December 5. Meanwhile the Russians proceeded to counterattack along the whole front. The Soviet actions brought the German army, which was not sufficiently equipped for wintertime fighting, into a serious state of crisis. In this situation, Hitler's order was not to give up a single foot of territory. It was his relentless energy in urging this order to be carried out that kept the front from caving in, despite severe set-backs.

The summer of 1942 brought new German successes: The German troops pushed forward to Stalingrad and to the Caucasus, while in Africa Rommel was reaching the so-called El Alamein line, the last British defense concentration between him and Egypt. But, just as in the autumn of 1941 neither Leningrad nor Moscow could be taken, this new German offensive came to a halt without attaining its goals. The German forces never managed to occupy more than two-thirds of Stalingrad, nor did the Baku oil-fields fall to their advance. What is more, Germany's strength was already being strained to the utmost simply to maintain this – geographically greatest – extension of the various fronts. The limits of Germany's human and material capacity were reached at a time when her foes were just beginning to mobilize their own strength.

Since 1939, the United States had lent economic support to the British, and later in an increasing degree to the Soviet war effort. It did so first within the limits of the Neutrality Laws of 1935–36, and later on the basis of the Lend Lease Law of March 11, 1941. The long expected entry of the United States into the war was triggered off by the Japanese raid on Pearl Harbor and the subsequent declaration of war by Germany and Italy. Now the physical resources of the entire world could be mobilized against Germany. An abundance of war material of every sort could be turned out in industrial areas far distant from any German interference, or even from any German influence worth mentioning. By contrast, within Hitler's sphere of power there would soon be no longer any region in which production could go on free from air raids. And every loss of territory meant an irreplaceable loss of potential raw materials.

Politically, the American entry into the war meant a fusion of two fronts. It could only have been otherwise if, in 1940–41, a genuine alternative had still presented itself to Hitler whether to choose to push on against England or to attack Russia; or if the British and the Soviets had been so inalienably at odds, and simultaneously so much occupied with their immediate problems, that closer co-operation between London and Moscow was out of the question. None of this was the case. As a result, America now represented a supply base for both Great Britain and the Soviet Union. Furthermore, America was politically the connecting link. Economically and politically, conditions were ripe for the Allies to close ranks, ready to take the offensive in every theater of war. The British moved over to the attack at El Alamein on October 23, 1942. British and American troops landed in northwest Africa on November 7. The Russians on November 19 started their action that was to draw a noose around the German Sixth Army in Stalingrad. In a nutshell, the military initiative went over to the Allies, and Hitler saw himself forced onto the defensive.

Against this coalition of three world powers, Germany's champion was Adolf Hitler – thanks to the system of absolutism that had meanwhile been perfected within his borders. The embattled land looked to the capacities and decisions of one man. But the Führer had always considered politics as nothing more or less than a struggle for power. In this struggle, as he conceived it, all that mattered were force of will and tactical skill. He had never seen nor practiced politics as "the art of the possible". As for actual warfare, to Hitler it was not a political problem at all. He concentrated his attention and energy almost exclusively on the military phases of the campaigns. This was particularly clear in his attitude toward the army high command, the ultimate leadership of which he took into his own hands at the end of 1941. The more he lost himself in a widening maze of purely technical and tactical matters, the more he let the domestic situation of his Reich move toward chaos. Internationally, he was blind towards the possibility of using his foreign policy to improve Germany's military situation or to ease the predicament of her fighting men. He simply did not have the statesmanlike imagination to meet the world-wide conflict with a positive political concept – or even to make advantageous use of those political factors that were already inherent in the situation. Indeed, he went so far as to cut the ties that others had spun. Why so "unpolitical"? Because he was convinced – judging others by his knowledge of himself – that everything that was not a trick or an act of force could only be interpreted as a sign of weakness. Once, after the campaign in France, he had shown that he was unable to use the methods of diplomacy in order to forge a coalition against Great Britain. In the same way, at this later stage in the war, he failed to grasp the chances that were at hand: opportunities for Germany that could be realized, for example, by skilful diplomacy in the Near East; or by a farsighted treatment of the defeated nations of Western Europe.

Goebbels perceived this failing in Hitler, and formulated it when he wrote in his diary in 1943: "We are waging too much war and too little politics. Under present circumstances, at a time when our military successes are not particularly great, we would do well to learn once more how to handle the political instrument."

Nowhere did Hitler gamble away political potentialities more recklessly than in his administration of the occupied Eastern territories. Theoretically, he might have made use of the reservoir of good will that Germany enjoyed among peoples whom the German advance had freed from the Communist yoke. Theoretically, he could have seen to it that his regime offered those peoples an example of humane policy and sound administration. Such behavior might have linked them to the Reich in ties of friendship. But instead of seeking to win them, Hitler categorized them as "sub-human races", and subjected them to the crude exploitation of a type of colonialism that was going out all over the world. Such policies as Hitler had were self-defeating. For example, he permitted a propaganda campaign for the autonomy of the Ukraine, but only as long as such a campaign was good tactics. In almost the same breath he ensured that his propaganda gesture would bring on no practical consequences. As he saw it, his German soldiers had not overrun the territories in question for the purpose of fostering an autonomous nation in the Ukraine, but purely in order to win their Führer's indispensable "Lebensraum". As for the suggestion that Germany might benefit by fostering the build-up of a Russian fighting force composed of the anti-Bolshevist adherents of Wlassow, Hitler dismissed it as "a fantasy of the first degree of magnitude".

There was open debate about the policy or non-policy in the Ukraine. Alfred Rosenberg and the Reich Commissioner Erich Koch had a discussion about it in Hitler's presence in 1943. Rosenberg was for founding "national committees" and national academies and for creating the foundations of an independent state. Koch retorted that Rosenberg was out of touch with the realities. Koch asked ironically: When the army requested him to deliver 5,700,000 tons of grain, could he reply that he was sorry; that since he had to build up a nice clean Ukrainian state, he could let the army have only one or two million tons of grain? And how was Koch to send Ukrainians to academies? He had "lost" 500,000 Jews who had been skilled workers, and he needed the Ukrainians to mend boots. Rosenberg, Koch continued, was living in a pretty world of organization, but Koch had the down-to-earth job of satisfying a thousand demands – and that was the job he was going to do. From his own standpoint, Koch was right, and most of the facts spoke for him.

For the truth was that the enormous military efforts (if one disregards the additional consequences that resulted from the annihilation of the Jews, mentioned by Koch) had eaten away Germany's reserves; had consumed those reserves at such a rate, in fact, that everything that came to hand had to be used exclusively to fill an immediate need. In other words, practically speaking, there was no possibility to employ such resources to pursue political goals calculated to preserve German hegemony in the long run. And yet the German dilemma in this regard was the logical result of Hitler's decision in 1936 – in which he resolved in advance to overdraw Germany's reserves, counting on redressing the balance by utilizing the resources of the "Lebensraum" still to be conquered. Koch's "practical" policy about the resources was directly in line with this strategy. It was a strategy that had first led to a fantastic series of successes and now was beginning to defeat itself. For his part, Rosenberg, and quite a few other National Socialist leaders who more or less forcefully opposed this so obviously abortive "East policy", were right – in principle. But in practice, their ideas were utopian as measured by the actual situation. The unadorned policy of power, in its extravagance, was turning Hitler's war into a naked battle of survival, even before the German fronts began to give way in the face of enemy attacks.

With the progressive deterioration of the situation, Hitler's military and political errors became so apparent that there was a growing amount of sharp criticism in the ranks of leading National Socialists. Much of this opposition was based doubtlessly on true insights and genuine concern. But the critics were of little practical service. For their awareness that things were going wrong dealt only with symptoms. The reason why the critics did not see the underlying cause of the German failures was simply that this underlying

cause was the strategy of Hitler; and the opposi-
tionists among the National Socialists distanced
themselves only from the failures and not from
most of Hitler's premises. His premises they accepted more or less as they always had. Besides,
National Socialists who knew that mistakes were
being made considered it self-evident that the war
had to be won before basic reforms could be carried out. Yet the basic reforms – had they been possible – were the only way to prevent military
catastrophe. As early as 1943, the question was
no longer whether Germany would win or lose,
but whether the inevitable defeat would amount
to complete destruction as well.

During the course of the year 1944, at the
latest, it became clear that if Hitler could not
carry off a victory, he would not shrink from
abandoning his nation and his countrymen to
complete annihilation. During the crisis of the
winter of 1941/42 he had turned out to be right,
in a military sense, when he insisted on the defense of every foot of territory. Now, accordingly,
he made the same doctrine, of holding on at any
price, the fatal last word of his military wisdom.
He sacrificed valuable divisions rather than vo-
luntarily abandoned positions that could be held
no longer. He knew well that as things got
worse only the order not to give a single inch
could camouflage the situation. Any other tac-

86

tical measure would have immediately revealed that there was simply nothing militarily useful to be done any more. For by now Germany's strength would no longer suffice for her long-range defense. Nor was there strength enough to score a military advance that might have renewed the nation's dwindling resources. In other words: The war was lost. More and more, Hitler began to shut himself off from reality, and to ignore unpleasant facts. Anybody who still found the courage to present him with the situation as it really existed was branded a malevolent defeatist. As the outside world observed the approach of Germany's fate, Hitler withdrew into a private world of his wishes and demands.

Under these extraordinary circumstances, leaders of the German resistance to Hitler had to consider extraordinary means of removing him. They were means, it is true, that could be justified only in the completely abnormal situation that existed in Germany: where the destiny of a whole people had become dependent on the arbitrary will of one man who was on the brink of madness. More than that, he was a man who for his part had long since betrayed the trust of those who had pledged their allegiance to him. Here, then, lay the weak point in the German resistance: not that it took extraordinary means to liberate Germany from Hitler – but that this action was started so late. By the time the resistance struck its major blow, that blow seemed to represent only an attempt of averting the certain catastrophe, rather than an attempt of liberating Germany from a rule that was unworthy of her.

The failure of the plot of July 20, 1944, fortified Hitler in his sense of mission, and once and for all justified, in his own mind, his distrust of the armed forces and of officialdom. In his madly distorted imagination, Germany had returned to what he remembered as "the days of struggle" before 1933. As he saw it, cowards and traitors were at work to hand over Germany to her enemies, while he, relying solely on the loyal members of his movement, was fighting a desperate fight for the future of the German people. Furthermore, he now considered the National Socialist movement alone to be the true representative of the German will to fight, the standard-bearer of the struggle for Germany's destiny. So he entrusted the future organization of the war effort exclusively to his closest henchmen. Himmler took over not only the command of the reserve army – and with it of course the power of disposition over this reservoir of combat strength – but even temporarily the command of an actual army group. This latter enterprise, however, soon became a fiasco.

After "total war" had been proclaimed in February 1943 as a reaction to the Allied decisions announced at Casablanca, in August 1944 Goebbels became Commissioner General for this intensified war effort. Bormann and Himmler were charged with organizing the concept known as "the German people in arms" – the *Volkssturm* – and both competed with Goebbels in the organization of the *Werwolf*. More than all others, this "Werwolf" operation, aiming at action behind the enemy's lines, was an illusionary manoeuvre – and in so far as it became reality, it was both senseless and criminal. Hitler's demands became more and more fantastic, his orders constantly more arbitrary. But whoever could not comply with them, or did not want to comply with them, from a feeling of responsibility for the human beings entrusted to him, was considered a traitor. The severity of the military penal code was increased to the point of absurdity: Now the laws no longer served their real purpose, that of discipline and order at the front, but instead they began producing a legal situation of such insecurity that prudent and responsible action was rendered almost impossible. And the quandary of conscience became complete.

On March 20, 1945, Hitler issued an order to destroy all such military installations – whether involving traffic, communication, industrial production or supply – as well as all such capital goods within the area of the Reich as the enemy could in some way utilize for fighting purposes. On hearing of this order, no less a personage than Albert Speer spoke up. It was Speer who had succeeded, despite the increasing aerial bombardment, in preventing a breakdown of German armament facilities. Now Speer told Hitler that the scorched-earth order would not work any serious disadvantages on the enemy, but would deprive the German people of even the most rudimentary foundations for continuing their existence. Speer announced that therefore he would do everything he could to blunt the purpose of Hitler's order. To that Hitler replied that if the war was going to be lost, the people would be lost as well; so it was not necessary to be concerned with the fundamentals that the people would need for their continued existence. In any event, continued Hitler, the German people had proved itself to be the weaker, and the future belonged exclusively to the stronger people of the East. Those who survived the fighting, he added, would be anyhow only the inferior ones.

With collapse staring them in the face, the German people fought on. They fought on in the East in the desperate attempt to save as large a part of Germany as possible from Russian occupation; and in the West because nobody dared on his own initiative to put an end to the senseless resistance. There still remained the semblance of a possibility of giving a different turn to the war: first, the thought of miracle weapons, and, secondly, the idea that discord might break out among the Allies. These shadows of chances sufficed to preserve the hypnotic spell of obedience and the demonic overlordship of total rule until the last days. Only a few were capable of overcoming their trust in – or their fear of – Hitler's luck which had so often and astonishingly held out. Who was completely certain that no unforeseen turn of events would come? And if it did, who would want to be standing on the wrong side? In reality, however, Germany had no weapon at the end of the war that could have been compared with the atomic bomb, which was already available to the Americans, ready for use. And as far as a falling-out among the Allies was concerned, one cannot deny a political prescience to certain utterances of Hitler about the future development of their relations, as seen from today's perspective. However, Hitler failed to take into consideration the lesson of history, that an alliance of unlike partners tends to hold fast as long as they have not yet overcome a mutual enemy. Hitler had to experience the reality that with Roosevelt's unlooked-for death on April 12, 1945, the »miracle of the House of Brandenburg«[1] was not repeating itself for the Führer.

During the agony of the Third Reich, the National Socialist movement itself finally broke up. It broke up because of Hitler's egocentric resolve to drag Germany along with himself into the chasm of total defeat. It broke up because of the conflict between Hitler's delusions and reality; and in some cases because of the conflict between his delusions and a residue of realism that some of the highest National Socialist Leaders retained. When Sepp Dietrich – who had been a member of Hitler's personal guard as early as the year 1923 – found himself forced to withdraw to Vienna with his 6th Armored Army in April 1945, Hitler telegraphed him to this effect: The troops had failed to fight in the way that the situation demanded, and accordingly the SS divisions "Adolf Hitler", "Das Reich", "Totenkopf" and "Hohenstaufen" were to shed their stripes. A little later, Hitler expelled Göring and Himmler from the party because, he said, they had inflicted immeasurable damage on the country and on the people by secret negotiations with the enemy as well as by an attempt to usurp the power of the state. Hitler handed down this decree because

---

[1] In the Seven Years' War, Frederick the Great – despite a series of brilliant victories – was saved from final defeat only by the unexpected death of the Tsarina Elisabeth of Russia in 1762.

Göring and Himmler – in contrast to Goebbels and Bormann, who had eliminated from their considerations any concern for the fate of the people – had tried still to save something.

In these final hours, both the inherent perversity and the structural absurdity of the system were manifesting themselves for the last time. Once again the National Socialist system was proving able to create within itself paradox without precedent. Consider: He was branded as a traitor to Germany who, when forced to choose, chose for Germany instead of for a Führer who, while identifying himself with Germany, was preparing to sacrifice that country to his own obstinacy. The whole system had already sealed the fate of countless men and women of good will and exemplary patriotism. Now the nature of the system was being illuminated more garishly than ever, as in a final and brightest rocket-glare. The illumination came from Hitler's eleventh-hour attitude towards two men to whom he owed much; two men in fact who shared to a immense degree in the guilt for Germany's tragedy. Thus National Socialism, after wreaking untold harm on Germans and on others around the world, brought on the final catastrophe. The end had been foreseen by all who had remained clear-eyed enough to discriminate between falsity and truth, between right and wrong.

This brief history of the Third Reich first appeared, under the title "Grundlagen und politische Entwicklung des Dritten Reiches", in a handbook of the Federal Defense Ministry for education in history and current affairs. The handbook, "Schicksalsfragen der Gegenwart", is used in the orientation of members of the armed forces. This revised edition of the above-mentioned text is published by permission of the Federal Defense Ministry.

Chronology

| Oct. 23/24 | Hitler meets with Franco and Pétain, respectively |
| Oct. 28 | Italy starts war on Greece |

1941

March 11	Lend-Lease Treaty between United States and Great Britain goes into effect
March 21	Italo-German counterattack in North Africa
April 6	Start of the Balkan campaign
May 12	Bormann becomes chief of the party secretariat
June 22	Hitler starts war on the Soviet Union
Dec. 11	German declaration of war on the United States

1942

Jan. 20	Wannsee Conference: Beginning of the "final solution of the Jewish question"
Early Nov.	German defeat at El Alamein
Nov. 8	Landing of British and American troops in Morocco and Algeria

1943

| Jan. 31 | German troops surrender in Stalingrad |
| July 25 | Overthrow of Mussolini |

1944

June 6	Allied invasion of northern France
July 20	High-water mark of the German resistance: Count Stauffenberg's attempt to assassinate Hitler
Sept. 11	American troops cross the German border

1945

| April 30 | Hitler commits suicide |
| May 8 | Signing of the German surrender |

Bullock, Alan: Hitler. A study in tyranny. – London: Odhams Pr. 1952. 776 pp.; illus.

Crankshaw, Edward: Gestapo. Instrument of tyranny. – London: Putnam 1956. 275 pp.

Dallin, Alexander: German Rule in Russia. 1941–1945. A study of occupation policies. – London, New York: Macmillan 1957. XX, 695 pp.

Documents on German foreign policy 1918–1945. Ser. C: 1933–1937. Vol. 1–3. – Ser. D: 1937–1945. Vol. 1–10. – Washington: U.S. Govt. Printing Office; London: H. M. Stationery Office 1949 ff.

Heiden, Konrad: Der Führer. Hitler's Rise to Power. – London: Gollancz 1944. 614 pp.

Journal of Central European Affairs. Managing ed.: S. Harrison Thomson. Publ. quarterly at the University of Colorado. – Boulder/Colorado: Univ. of Colorado 1941 ff.

Mau, Hermann and Helmut Krausnick: German History 1933–45. An Assessment by German Historians. – London: Oswald Wolff (Publ.) Ltd. 1959

The Third Reich. Publ. under the auspices of the International Council for Philosophy and Humanistic Studies and with the assistance of UNESCO. – London: Weidenfeld and Nicolson 1955. XV, 910 pp.

Reichmann, Eva Gabriele: Hostages of Civilisation. The social sources of National Socialist anti-Semitism. – London: Gollancz 1950. 281 pp.

Rothfels, Hans: The German Opposition to Hitler. – London: Oswald Wolff (Publ.) Ltd. 1961. 170 pp.

Schlabrendorff, Fabian von: Revolt Against Hitler. A personal account. – London: Eyre and Spottiswoode 1948. XVIII, 176 pp.

Trevor-Roper, Hugh Redwald: The Last Days of Hitler. – London: Macmillan 1947. XII, 280 pp.

Wheeler-Bennett, John: The Nemesis of Power. The German army in politics 1918–1945. London: Macmillan 1953. XVI, 829 pp.; illus.